CONTENTS

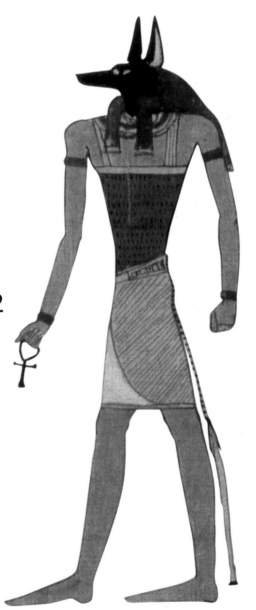

1 The Feast of Opet

'Halt!' The guard swung his spear across Tuyu's path. 'Sorry, lady,' he said, 'no one is allowed past Horemheb's Pylon. Orders.'

'I think you will find I am allowed in,' said Tuyu calmly. 'Myself and my two daughters.' Standing behind their mother, Teti and Meryt looked at each other and smiled. There was always some stupid guard who didn't recognize them.

Pesshut, one of Tuyu's slaves, went up to the guard. 'It's the Lady Tuyu, you fool! Let her through!' he shouted.

Into the temple

The guard glanced at Tuyu, who nodded graciously. Immediately, he raised his spear and sprang to attention. 'Lady Tuyu,' he pleaded, 'please accept my apologies.'

'You were only doing your duty,' she smiled, sweeping past him into the cool shade of the pylon. Trying their best to look dignified, Teti and Meryt followed.

The ruins of Amun's temple at Karnak are awe-inspiring even today. In ancient times the temple was truly magnificent.

The girls stared about them in silent wonder at the gigantic buildings, carvings and statues that towered above them on every side.

'I'm frightened!'

Meryt grasped her elder sister's hand. 'I'm frightened, Teti,' she whispered. 'It's all so, so *enormous*. It makes me feel like an ant.'

'Don't worry,' replied Teti. 'Compared with the Mighty Amun we are all ants. Even Dad.' She sounded grown-up, but actually she too was a bit frightened She was glad Meryt had taken her hand.

They were interrupted by their mother. 'Come along, you two,' she called. 'We must get to our positions before the procession begins or we'll miss the ceremony.' Leading the way, she took them through more courtyards, down cool corridors and, finally, up a long flight of stone steps to the roof of the Outer Pylon.

A small statue of the god Amun which was probably made during the reign of King Tutankhamun, in the fourteenth century BC.

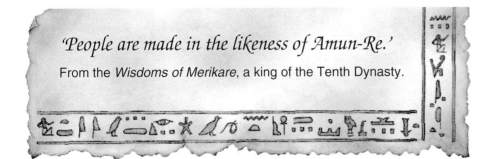

'People are made in the likeness of Amun-Re.'

From the *Wisdoms of Merikare*, a king of the Tenth Dynasty.

The Outer Pylon

The view was fantastic. To the west, the mighty Nile ran broad and blue in the early morning light. A tree-lined canal linked the river to a large lake. On every other side, the temple of Karnak sprawled like a small town. Its shrines, sphinxes, pylons, obelisks, statues and other buildings were encircled by a high brick wall.

Tuyu pointed to a tall stone building. 'That's where the procession starts,' she explained. 'Then it winds through the streets to this pylon and ends up at the landing stage over there.'

She pointed to a golden barge moored beside the lake. 'That's *Userhat*, the boat that will take the god upstream to Luxor.'

A model of the boat that held the god's statue when he travelled down the Nile.

The unknowable

A loud drum roll announced the start of the ceremony. Soon afterwards, the procession came into view. First came guards, clearing a path through the crowds. They were followed by musicians playing harps, flutes, and clattering tambourines. Dancers and acrobats leaped about among them.

A line of priests in white robes came next. Then the boats appeared, decorated with gold, jewels and carvings and carried high on the shoulders of priests. In the most brilliant boat, with a ram's head on its bow, the statue of the Great God Amun sat behind a curtain beneath a golden canopy.

'Why can't we see him?' whispered Teti.

'Sh-h-h!' said her mother quietly. 'He's Unknowable, that's why.'

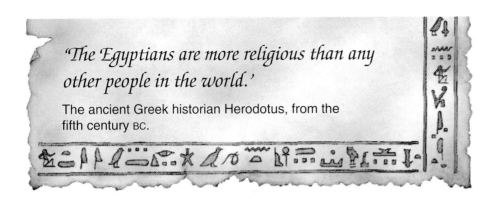

'The Egyptians are more religious than any other people in the world.'

The ancient Greek historian Herodotus, from the fifth century BC.

Userhat

The procession passed down a road lined with sphinxes to the water's edge. Here the smaller boats were loaded onto larger ones moored in the lake. When Amun was safely aboard *Userhat*, a team of men began to tow the boats down the canal towards the river.

Teti pointed to a priest sitting in the centre of *Userhat*. 'Who's that, Mum?' she asked. 'The man in the tall hat? He looks like Dad.'

Tuyu smiled. 'Looks like Dad? Maybe it's because it is Dad! Didn't you recognize him?'

Teti did not reply. Wow! she thought proudly. My Dad can almost touch the Unknowable. He must be really important.

The Avenue of Sphinxes at Karnak. Each creature had a lion's body and a male human head. In ancient Greece sphinxes were female.

2 The Egyptian Universe

The story of Meryt, Teti and their mother is set in ancient Egypt during the reign of King Rameses III, over 3,000 years ago. The ceremony they watched – the Opet Festival – took place every year in honour of the god Amun. We need a great deal of imagination to understand just how important festivals like this were.

Religion was vitally important to ancient Egypt. It explained everything that had happened and would happen in the future. The rising of the sun, harvest, illness, childbirth, cooking a meal – every aspect of life was controlled by the gods and goddesses. In the end, keeping them content was all that really mattered.

Changes and differences

The civilization of ancient Egypt existed for more than 3,000 years. During this time the popularity of the gods changed. The worship of Amun, for example, became very important during the New Kingdom period, from about 1550 to 1070 BC.

Egypt stretched more than 1,000 km along the valley of the Nile. Its regions had different gods and different ways of worship. For much of Egypt's history there were three main religious centres. Heliopolis, now part of modern Cairo, was the centre of sun god worship. At Memphis,

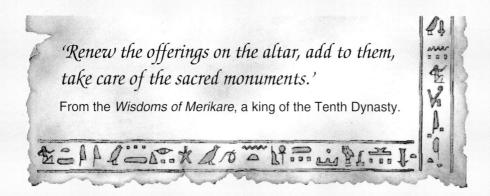

'Renew the offerings on the altar, add to them, take care of the sacred monuments.'

From the *Wisdoms of Merikare*, a king of the Tenth Dynasty.

further to the south, the creator god Ptah was most popular. The moon god Thoth was supreme at Hermopolis. Later, Osiris' temple at Abydos and Amun's at Karnak became very important.

Land and sky

Whichever gods and goddesses were important, the Egyptian view of the universe did not change. The Earth god, known as Geb, lay below the sky goddess, known as Nut. They were surrounded by the waters of chaos, called Nun.

The sun floated across this ocean in a boat. The sun god, Re, spent half his time sailing the heavens and the other half in a region called Duat (the Underworld). Duat was Nut's womb, from which the sun was born again each morning. It was also the place where demons, the souls of the damned and a gigantic serpent called Apep lived.

A map showing ancient Egypt during the New Kingdom (about 1550–1070 BC).

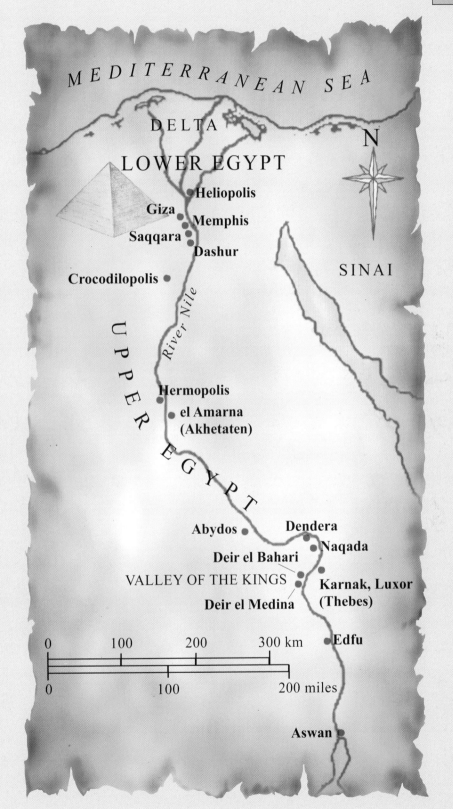

MEDITERRANEAN SEA

DELTA

LOWER EGYPT

N

Heliopolis
Giza
Memphis
Saqqara
Dashur

SINAI

Crocodilopolis

River Nile

UPPER EGYPT

Hermopolis
el Amarna
(Akhetaten)

Abydos   Dendera
          Naqada
Deir el Bahari
VALLEY OF THE KINGS
                  Karnak, Luxor
Deir el Medina   (Thebes)

0   100   200   300 km

0   100   200 miles

Edfu

Aswan

Order and chaos

The Egyptians believed their world was made up of opposites: night/day, male/female, flood/drought, life/death, order/chaos and so forth. The purpose of religion was to keep these opposites in balance.

The two most basic opposites were order and chaos. Order was divine – it came from the gods. Chaos was often man-made, and the Egyptians were terrified of it.

It is important to remember that the Egyptians' advanced civilization was unusual. Looking across their frontiers, they saw less civilized societies eager to smash Egypt's order and plunder its wealth. The annual flooding of the Nile, bringing new life to the parched soil along its banks, was another aspect of Egypt's sacred order.

Ma'at

In one myth the Egyptians believed that when the Creator (Atum) decided to make the universe, his first act was to lift up the young girl Ma'at and bring her to life with a kiss. Ma'at, the first-made, was the goddess of Truth and Justice. But more important than either of these, she was also the goddess of Universal Order.

The protection of Ma'at was a king's first duty. If he ruled in her name, he was bound to rule justly. To rebel against the king, therefore, was more than just a crime. It was heresy because it threatened Egypt's god-given order. And if that broke down, it broke down everywhere because Egypt was the whole world.

Isfet

Ordinary Egyptians were expected to preserve Ma'at by living just, honest and balanced lives. That meant working hard, not taking advantage of the weak, not stealing and living in harmony with the god-given environment.

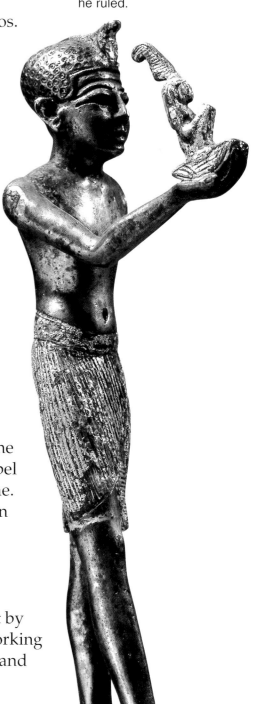

The king as the guardian of order. The statue shows a king holding a statue of Ma'at, the goddess of truth and order in whose name he ruled.

An illustration on a coffin showing the air god Shu separating the sky goddess Nut from the earth god Geb.

Because everyone knew about Ma'at, for most of their history the Egyptians did not feel it necessary to spell out their laws and commandments. But they did write many 'Books of Wisdom' that instructed people how to stay in tune with Ma'at.

The opposite of Ma'at was Isfet, or chaos. It existed outside Egypt and could, if people did not behave, enter the country. It came in the form of law-breaking, invasion, famine and plague.

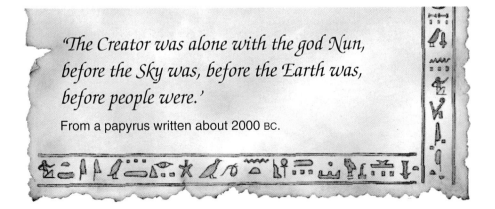

'The Creator was alone with the god Nun, before the Sky was, before the Earth was, before people were.'

From a papyrus written about 2000 BC.

Super-powers

We translate the Egyptian word *netjer* as 'god'. It is not a very accurate translation. When the Egyptians used the word *netjer* they had in mind a power that was non-human and above nature. As there is no single English word for this 'out-of-this-world' force, we have to make do with 'god' and 'goddess'.

From earliest times the Egyptians had an idea of a super-god, a sort of force-to-end-all-forces. This mysterious power was known as the 'Hidden One'.

All shapes and sizes

The Egyptians had literally dozens of gods and goddesses. Most originated in Egypt. To begin with they were linked to a specific region. Amun, for example, was associated with Thebes. In later times, when Egypt came into closer contact with other cultures, foreign deities were introduced. And Egyptian deities, especially the goddess Isis, became popular abroad. She was even popular in Britain by Roman times.

Amun aboard his heavenly boat with the sun disc and two baboons, representing wisdom.

No one could say what a god or goddess looked like because a power has no shape or form. But Egypt's deities appeared in guises that human beings could recognize. Isis, for example, was normally human. Re took the form of the sun or a falcon. Amun was usually human but might be a ram or a goose, and Sobek was a crocodile.

King-god

Egypt relied on its all-powerful king. Without him law and order broke down, the harvest was not organized and foreigners invaded. Not surprisingly, kings came to be seen as gods. We don't know whether this idea came from the king himself or from his people. It was probably a bit of both.

Djoser, who ruled from about 2667 to 2648 BC, was the first king who was also seen to be a god. He and his successors were said to be the falcon god Horus. As the falcon soared over the earth, so the king was above his kingdom. Later generations were less sure of the king's divinity during his lifetime, but they were certain he became a god after his death.

A medallion of the goddess Isis from the first century BC. Worship of the mother-goddess spread from Egypt all over the ancient world.

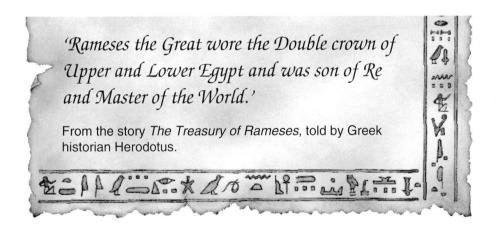

'Rameses the Great wore the Double crown of Upper and Lower Egypt and was son of Re and Master of the World.'

From the story *The Treasury of Rameses*, told by Greek historian Herodotus.

Temples

Unlike a Christian church or a Muslim mosque, a temple
was not a place where people gathered to worship.
Instead, it was a house for the deity to whom it was
dedicated. It was managed by priests and priestesses,
and ordinary people were not allowed inside.

There were two types of temple. The first was
dedicated to one of Egypt's many gods or goddesses.
The second, known as a 'mortuary temple', was dedicated
to the honour of a dead king, who had become a god.
Because kings controlled the country's wealth, many
of them constructed enormous mortuary temples before
they died.

Ritual

The Egyptians did not believe in progress. They thought
the world had been created perfect and it was their duty
to keep it so. This meant making sure that order was
maintained. To do this, all the gods had to be pleased
with rituals.

A ritual was a regular ceremony. It might be performed
every year, like the Opet Festival, or several times a day.
The most common ritual took place in the inner part of the

One of the temples of
Rameses the Great
(Rameses II), built over
3,200 years ago in
Abu Simbel.

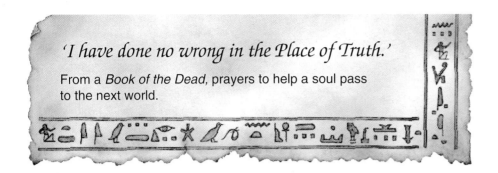

Bes, the popular household god, dancing with a tambourine.

temple where the image of the deity was kept. The image was not the deity itself, but their spirit lived in it. During a normal ritual, priests washed the image, dressed it in clean clothes and left it food.

At home with the gods

Not all rituals took place in temples. Ordinary homes had little shrines where household deities were honoured. These included the spirits of ancestors and the popular dwarf-god Bes, who helped with childbirth. Carvings of household deities could be found all over the home, even on make-up jars.

The Egyptians' mysterious religion was closely mixed up with magic, spirits and demons. Spells and special rituals were used to keep these forces of evil at bay. There were also magic spells to bring good luck at almost every occasion. The right spell could hasten recovery from sickness, for example, or help a woman get pregnant, or protect a soldier from injury in battle.

3 The Deities

Egyptian civilization emerged along the fertile strip beside the River Nile over 7,000 years ago. By civilization we mean three things: living in settled communities, doing specialist work (for example, farming and carpentry), and getting food from agriculture rather than hunting and gathering.

For about 2,000 years the Nile valley was dotted with dozens of small, independent communities. Each had its own gods and goddesses. Over time, powerful kings gradually joined the Nile communities together into two kingdoms, Upper and Lower Egypt. Finally, around 3100 BC, King Namer united all Egypt into a single kingdom. The local deities remained, however. This is why Egypt's gods and goddesses were so many and so varied.

A Middle Kingdom statue of a hippopotamus. The creature's form was taken by the goddess of childbirth, Taweret.

Nature worship

Like all early peoples, the early Egyptians were very much part of the natural world. There was no distinction between humans and nature. The sun, the stars, the river, animals and birds, together with people, all shared the same existence. And they were all equally respected.

So when the Egyptians thought about the powers that controlled their world – gods and goddesses – they automatically linked them to everyday things they admired or feared. The ram, for example, was supposed to be always wanting to reproduce. So the people of Elephantine saw their creator god, Khnum, as a ram. That is how many deities came to be represented in animal form.

National gods

Although Egypt remained a land of local gods and goddesses, some deities became accepted everywhere. The chief of these was the king himself, who was the falcon god Horus in human form. Because the king ruled all Egypt, so Horus was a national god.

From about 1500 BC onwards, Amun was another national god. When the rulers of the New Kingdom started favouring him, he became the country's chief god. He was often joined to the sun god as Amun-Re.

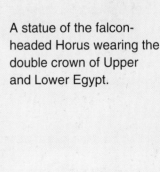

A statue of the falcon-headed Horus wearing the double crown of Upper and Lower Egypt.

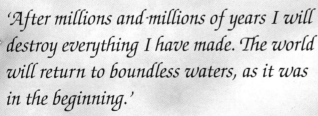

'*After millions and millions of years I will destroy everything I have made. The world will return to boundless waters, as it was in the beginning.*'

The prophecy of the god Amun in a *Book of the Dead*.

Changing sun

Egyptian gods could be more than one thing at the same time. Although we find this rather confusing, it was actually quite logical. It arose because the natural forces of the Earth also take many forms.

The sun, for example, is not just a fixed light in the sky. It rises and sets, changes colour, provides heat and light, makes crops grow and brings drought. The sun is all-powerful because it makes life possible – yet it 'dies' every day.

The Egyptians adapted their religion to tie in with what they saw. So the sun itself (Re) was not normally a god on its own. Instead, it was a form that several deities could take.

The forms of Re

The Eye of Re was a goddess, daughter of the sun god whom she protected. The rising sun was another god, Khepri. Its symbol was a beetle that laid its eggs in a ball of dung. This, like the rising sun, was a symbol of rebirth. The setting sun was Atum-Re, the creator of the universe.

As the sun ruled creation, so the king (Horus) ruled the earth. The falcon god Horus became linked to the sun as Re-Harakhte ('Ruler of the Horizon'). Amun showed himself in the sun as Amun-Re. Finally, there was Aten, the disc or circle of the sun which let light into the world.

The Aten Heresy

All Egypt's kings except one had roughly the same beliefs. The exception was King Amenhotep IV (about 1353–1336 BC). After ruling for four years, he changed his name to Akhenaten, meaning 'Working for Aten'.

Beetle power – a jewelled chest panel from the Twenty-first Dynasty showing the god Khepri, a scarab beetle, as the rising sun.

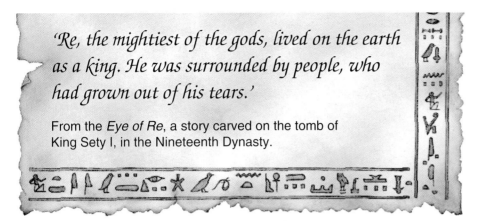

'Re, the mightiest of the gods, lived on the earth as a king. He was surrounded by people, who had grown out of his tears.'

From the *Eye of Re*, a story carved on the tomb of King Sety I, in the Nineteenth Dynasty.

The change marked a new form of religion. Instead of the traditional jumble of gods and goddesses, Akhenaten recognized one supreme god: Light, which came through the sun disc Aten. Light itself could not be shown, although it was all-powerful.

Akhenaten's successors swiftly wiped out the new religion and returned to the old ways. But some scholars believe that the Jewish idea of one god (later adopted by Christians and Muslims) had its roots in Akhenaten's heresy.

Akhenaten the heretic. The king, here offering lotus flowers to the sun disc, made the sun god Aten supreme over all others. The new-style worship may have influenced later religions.

The Main Gods and Goddesses of Ancient Egypt

AMUN The 'Hidden One'; originally from Thebes; later the most important national god; became the Roman god Jupiter; in the form of a ram or a goose.

ANHUR Sun god; later a god of war.

ANUBIS God of mummification; assisted entry into the underworld; in the form of a jackal.

APIS Ancient bull god associated with Ptah.

ASH Ancient god of the desert associated with Seth.

ATEN Sun disc god through whom Light shone.

ATUM The Creator.

BES Popular household god; helped with childbirth; in the form of an ugly dwarf.

BASTET Cat goddess worshipped in the Nile delta.

GEB Earth god married to Nut; father of Osiris, Isis, Seth and Nephthys.

HAPY Nile god.

HATHOR Goddess of love, happiness, dance and music; decided a child's future; associated with Isis; in the form of a cow.

HEH Frog god of eternity.

HORAKHTY Sun god (Re) at dawn; associated with the Sphinx.

HORUS Ancient sky god; later, son of Osiris and Isis; reigned as King of Egypt; often associated with Re; form of a falcon.

ISIS Sister-wife of Osiris; mother of Horus; great magical powers; guardian of children; human in form.

KHEPRI Sun god (Re) in beetle form.

KHNUM Ram god of Elephantine.

MA'AT Goddess of truth, justice and order; human form.

MERTSAGER Snake goddess.

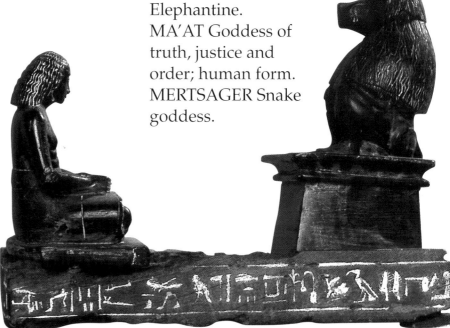

Learning from the master – a scribe sits before the baboon god Thoth, the inventor of writing.

MESKHENT Goddess of childbirth.
MONTU Soldier god of Thebes; in the form of a falcon or a bull.
MUT Goddess of Thebes; in the form of a lioness or vulture.
NEITH Warrior goddess from northern Egypt.
NEKHBET Vulture goddess of Upper Egypt.
NEPHTHYS Sister of Isis; sister-wife of Seth; human in form.
NUN God of the waters from which the first gods were born.
NUT Sky goddess who swallowed the sun (Re) every evening and gave birth to him each morning.
OSIRIS Husband-brother of Isis; god of earth, crops; ruler of the underworld; the annual flooding of the Nile was a symbol of his rebirth; kings became Osiris when they died; human in form.
PTAH Ancient Memphis creator god of craftsmen; gave everything in the world its name; usually human in form, but as a mummy.
RE The sun or sun god; originally from Heliopolis; Egyptians were the 'cattle of Re'; in the form of a ram, a falcon or a man.
SEKHMET Lioness goddess and bringer of plague and destruction.
SELKET Scorpion goddess; guarded kings' coffins.
SETH Brother (and later murderer) of Osiris; Lord of Upper Egypt; god of deserts, storms and chaos; in the form of a large-eared, imaginary animal.
SOBEK Crocodile god representing royal might; main temple in Crocodopolis.
TAWERET Hippopotamus goddess; oversaw pregnancy and childbirth.
THOTH God of wisdom and the moon; brought the arts to human beings; in the form of an ibis or baboon.
WADJET Cobra goddess; protected the king.

'The Kingdom of Osiris is a dismal and gloomy wasteland of sand.'

From *The Journey of Re*, a story carved on the tomb of King Sety I of the Nineteenth Dynasty.

Mother and child – such images of Isis and her infant son Horus may have influenced Christian ideas of the Virgin Mary and the baby Jesus.

4 Temples and Priests

The main purpose of a temple was to act as a home for a god or goddess. Obviously, because they were a force rather than a person, they did not actually live anywhere. But their statue was kept in the temple, which meant their spirit was there too.

In temples dedicated to a former king (mortuary temples) the statue was normally of the king-god himself. Statues of other gods and goddesses were either all human or human with an animal head. Anubis, for example, had a jackal head. The temples of some of the animal gods, such as Sobek the crocodile, kept real live animals as well as statues.

Temple buildings

Most large temples had roughly the same arrangement of rooms. The entrance was a pylon – a gateway made of two sloping-sided uprights with a beam across the top.

A diagram of the central part of the great temple at Karnak. It expanded greatly in the New Kingdom period as many kings built more monuments there.

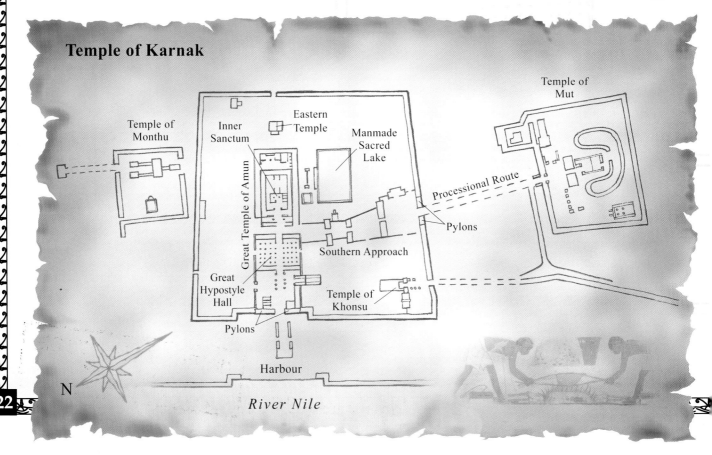

Temple of Karnak

Temple of Monthu

Temple of Mut

Inner Sanctum

Eastern Temple

Manmade Sacred Lake

Great Temple of Amun

Processional Route

Pylons

Southern Approach

Great Hypostyle Hall

Temple of Khonsu

Pylons

N

Harbour

River Nile

Beyond this was an open courtyard with columns round the outside. This led to a large hall, then the inner sanctum – the chamber where the statue of the god was kept. The buildings were of costly but long-lasting stone.

Around the temple itself clustered many smaller buildings. These included the priest's houses, kitchens, a sacred pool, a granary, and several stores for food and other necessities.

Wealth of the temples

There was no money in ancient Egypt. Those who built the temples and pyramids were paid in food, cloth or other necessities. If the king was building the temple, these came from the royal store houses where taxes were collected. Other temples were built by volunteers or the cult's own funds.

Temples grew rich through gifts that were intended to win the favour of the god or goddess. In the New Kingdom some temples became vastly wealthy. They owned lands and towns. A few had fleets of ships that traded with other lands.

Karnak

Karnak temple was the largest in all Egypt. The main complex, about 450 x 400 metres, was arranged east-west along the path of the sun. It had two harbours on man-made lakes that were linked to the Nile by canal. As well as the main temple of Amun, there were lesser temples dedicated to Mut and Khonsu (Amun's wife and son) and an Opet Festival shrine.

All the great kings of the New Kingdom added to Karnak's glory. Thutmose I and III, Amenhotep III and Hatshepsut constructed gigantic pylons and obelisks. Amenhotep II, Thutmose III, Rameses II and III extended the temples. The Great Hypostyle Hall, a forest of 134 carved pillars, was the work of Sety I and finished off by his son Rameses II.

Daily ritual

The same temple ritual was performed three times every day, all over Egypt. It honoured the god and encouraged its spirit to remain in the temple statue. After washing and praying, a priest entered the god's sanctuary. Choirs sang and the smell of incense wafted through the air.

The priest lit a torch to wake the god. The statue was then taken down from its pedestal, undressed, washed and adorned with clean clothes, make-up and jewellery. When it was back in place, food was placed before it. With more chants and incense, the priest begged the spirit of the god to enjoy the meal. The priest and his helpers then left the sanctuary and sealed its door.

The glory of Karnak. Originally all the columns soared into the sky like this one in the first courtyard.

'After the sun-god Re had left the world, his throne passed to Osiris who reigned as a mortal king.'

The beginning of the story of *Osiris and Isis*.

Festivals

The Opet Festival was only one of several important religious festivals. At all of them, religious activities were accompanied by general merrymaking.

The Festival of the Beautiful Embrace celebrated the marriage of Horus and Hathor. Hathor was taken upstream on the 'Mistress of Love' boat to Horus' temple at Edfu. Here the mysterious embrace took place, symbolizing the creation of new human life. The Abydos Festival re-told the story of Isis and Osiris with drama and pageantry. Abydos, where Osiris' head was supposed to have been buried, was a popular place of pilgrimage.

Rameses II in the first courtyard at Karnak. Before him stands his daughter Bentanta.

Priests

In theory the king was the chief priest of every temple. All other priests – part-time and full-time – were his assistants. Part-timers were ordinary men who helped out in the temple for a few weeks each year then went back to their normal jobs. The full-timers (like Tuyu's husband) often came from priestly families whose temple position passed down from father to son. Some of these professional priests became very rich and powerful.

Professional priests wore special clothes and emblems. The cloak of the High Priest of Memphis, for example, was an animal skin covered in stars. All priests were expected to keep themselves scrupulously clean. This meant that they bathed twice a day and twice a night, and shaved their whole body, even their eyebrows and eyelashes!

Priestesses

In the early days both men and women were priests. The goddess Hathor, for instance, was served almost entirely by priestesses. By the New Kingdom, however, temples were managed by male priests. Women still played an important part by acting as temple musicians.

The one exception to the all-male rule was 'God's Wife of Amun'. This was a leading female member of the royal family, usually the king's daughter. The job of a God's Wife was to use her female charm to keep Amun happy. Pictures in the temple at Karnak show the God's Wife being embraced by contented gods.

Petamenope, a chief priest and scribe at Karnak about 650 BC. The sculpture is a deliberate attempt to return to the Old Kingdom style of nearly 2,000 years earlier.

Everyday religion

Although most Egyptians did not take part in priestly rituals, they could participate in other religious activities. For example, they had their own household shrines and gods. They also joined in the festivals. Most temples had a public shrine where locals could pray or leave offerings for the deity. At Karnak, Amun's public shrine was in the north wall of the temple.

The wearing of magical amulets was another religious practice. These were small jewels or ornaments that were supposed to keep off disease or evil spells. They came in all shapes – gods, animals and parts of the body – and were worn by the dead as well as the living.

Wailing women mourn the death of Vizier Ramose, Chief Minister of King Amenhotep III and Akhenaten.

'Ptah gave life to all the gods through his heart and his tongue.'

From a text known as the *Memphis Theology*.

'Re, the greatest of gods, reigned on earth as a mortal pharaoh.'

From the story of *Eye of Re* found in the tomb of Sety I.

5 The Life Hereafter

Ancient Egypt's greatest monuments, the pyramids, were huge tombs. The Egyptians preserved dead bodies as mummies and worshipped the dead. These and other strange customs can give the impression that the Egyptians were obsessed with death, the 'enemy'.

In fact, the opposite is true. They believed that, with luck and careful preparation, the dead went on living. Death was just a difficult doorway they had to go through. All the Egyptian customs connected with death were really ways of trying to keep life going.

Packing for eternal life

The dead needed things from this life in the next. So bodies were buried with clothes, jewellery and other possessions. The tombs of kings were packed with even more exotic objects, including chariots and boats. The first kings actually had their servants buried with them. Later, model servants called *shawabti* were used.

Life after death was granted only to those who passed all kinds of tests. To help them, the dead were buried with written instructions, prayers and spells, often from a *Book of the Dead*. When kings were buried in pyramids, their helpful words were carved on the walls of their tombs as 'pyramid texts'. Later, when the Egyptians believed that all kinds of people – not just kings – could have eternal life, the helpful words were carved on coffin lids or written on papyrus and placed in tombs or coffins.

A model ship from the New Kingdom. This was found in the tomb of Tutankhamun.

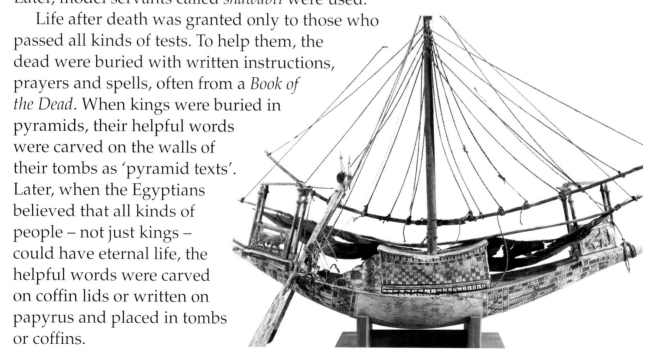

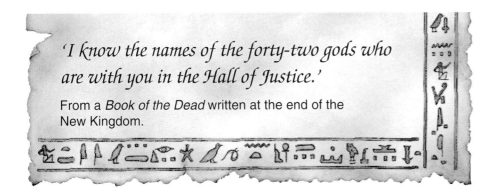

'I know the names of the forty-two gods who are with you in the Hall of Justice.'

From a *Book of the Dead* written at the end of the New Kingdom.

The Underworld

When a person died, their spirit left the body and went to the Underworld. This was the place of the setting sun, Osiris' gloomy kingdom under the Earth. It was a dark region of long corridors, bolted doorways and echoing halls. In shadowy corners lurked serpents and demons, waiting to ambush passers by.

Somehow, helped by the instructions buried with them, the dead had to find their way through the mazy Underworld to the Hall of Judgement. Whenever they came to a doorway, they had to know the name of the sinister doorkeeper or he would not let them through. If they forgot his name, they could wander about the Underworld for ever.

Weighing the heart in the Underworld. The jackal-headed Anubis weighs the heart of a dead person against the feather of Ma'at, or Truth.

In the balance

On reaching the Hall of Judgement, the dead had to remember exactly how they had got there – not only the names of the doorkeepers but even the number of bolts on their doors. If they passed this test, they were ready for judgement.

The judging was done by Osiris and his forty-two assistants. These represented Egypt's forty-two regions or 'nomes'. First, the dead person had to promise that they had not committed any sins during their life on earth. Then Anubis placed their heart on one side of a pair of scales. On the other side was a feather from the goddess Ma'at. The two had to balance exactly.

Success or failure

Terrible fates awaited those who failed the judgement. The worst sinners were sent for everlasting torture by demons, fiends and devils. The hearts of all sinners were tossed to the 'Swallowing Monster'(Ammut) – a frightening combination of a crocodile, lion and hippopotamus. Egyptians believed the heart was a person's 'self', the core of their personality. When the heart was swallowed they ceased to exist.

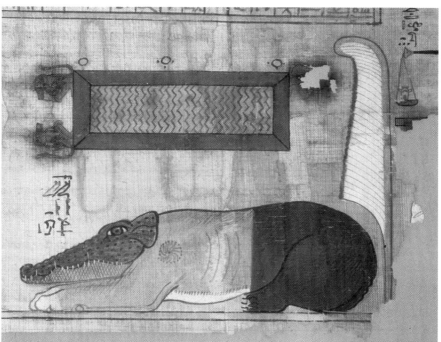

Food for the monster – the dreaded lion-crocodile-hippopotamus 'Swallowing Monster' waits in the Underworld to gulp up the souls of sinners.

Those who passed the test became holy spirits. They were part of Osiris and used his name – Tuyu would become 'Osiris Tuyu', for example. They could take many forms and could visit the living as ghosts.

Tombs and cults

To prevent their tombs being robbed of their valuable contents, New Kingdom rulers were buried in the secret Valley of the Kings. The tombs, together with tunnels, staircases, shafts and storerooms, were carved out of solid rock. The partly untouched tomb of Tutankhamun was discovered here in 1922.

As the holy dead were deities, the living established cults to worship them. The cults were based in mortuary temples, the finest of which is Queen Hatshepsut's near the Valley of the Kings. Royal and non-royal cults kept alive the memory of a holy spirit with prayers and offerings. It was common practice to write letters to the dead, too, asking how they were and whether they would help the living with their problems.

'I have not caused anyone pain; I have not made anyone hungry; I have not made anyone cry.'

From a *Book of the Dead* written at the end of the New Kingdom.

The Valley of the Kings, where many of Egypt's kings and queens were buried in tombs carved out of the solid rock.

Bodies for the afterlife

Mysteriously, a dead spirit still needed a body. It was vital, therefore, to preserve their corpse for the afterlife. This led to the extraordinary custom of mummification.

Very early in their history, the Egyptians noticed that bodies buried in the dry desert sand did not rot. Gradually, experimenting with different techniques, they managed to produce a corpse that would last virtually for ever. This was the mummy.

Mummification

Mummification took about seventy days. First, the corpse was cut open and the internal organs taken out. These were dried and stored in canopic jars. The brain was pulled out through the nose with a hook. Sometimes the heart was preserved separately before being put back in the body.

The empty corpse was now packed inside and out with natron salt (a powdery substance found in the desert). After forty days it was completely dried out. The natron salt was then removed and the corpse washed, then oils and perfumes were added. The inside was stuffed with a mixture of resin and linen, and the outside wrapped in bandages often hundreds of metres long.

A face was sometimes painted on the dried skin. More realistic faces were built up with plaster. Better still, a mask of the dead person was placed over the front of the skull. The mummy was now complete.

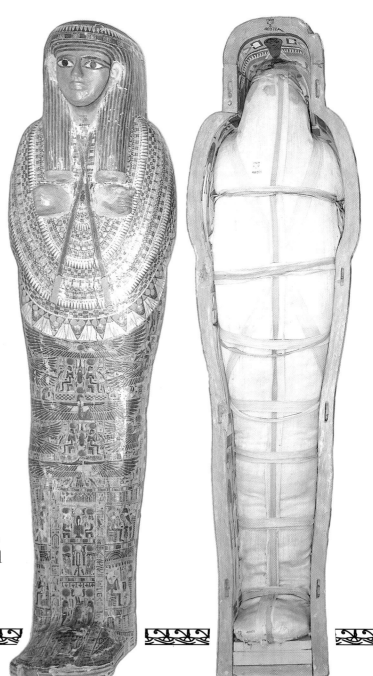

Preserved for ever: the mummified remains of an unknown priestess inside its brilliantly decorated mummy case, from about 1050 BC.

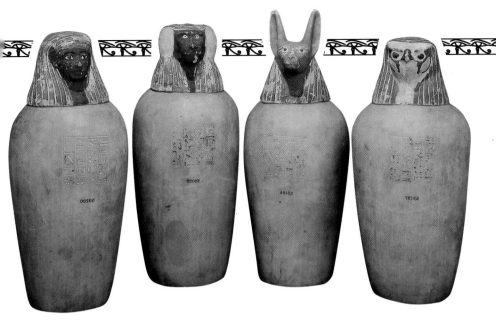

For use in the Afterlife: canopic jars in which internal organs, such as the stomach, lungs, liver and intestines, were stored beside the mummified body.

Beasts and curses

Certain animals were mummified as well as people. The favoured beasts were the animal gods: the holy crocodile of Crocodilopolis, the ibis of Hermopolis, the cat of Bastet and the bull of Memphis.

The dead were greatly upset if their tomb – the mummified body and its possessions – was disturbed. To scare off vandals, curses were occasionally written and placed inside tombs.

Lord Carnarvon, the sponsor of the Tutankhamun expedition, was said to have been the victim of such a curse when he died six months after the tomb was opened. And the Curse of Ankhmahor – that his mummy would wring the neck of anyone disturbing his tomb – has inspired dozens of horror movies.

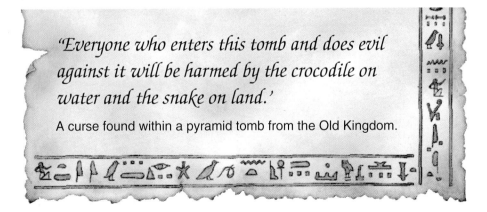

"Everyone who enters this tomb and does evil against it will be harmed by the crocodile on water and the snake on land.'

A curse found within a pyramid tomb from the Old Kingdom.

6 The Pyramids

Egypt's most impressive and famous monuments – the pyramids – are also among the oldest. They were built between about 2675 BC and 1630 BC. The largest were also some of the earliest, built in the Old Kingdom between about 2585 BC and 2510 BC.

Their construction is a remarkable achievement. The largest pyramid is King Khufu's at Giza. It is 146 metres tall and contains 2.3 million huge blocks of stone and was put up more than 4,500 years ago. It was built with soft metal tools and using only human labour. Each side rises at an angle of precisely 51° 52'. It is aligned exactly due north and the base is only 2.5 cm off a perfect square. Not surprisingly, it is regarded as one of the wonders of the world.

Egypt's own god

Most pyramids stand along a 40 km stretch of the Nile near Memphis. They are on the west bank of the river – the side of the setting (dying) sun. On a pyramid site were both the tomb of a king-god and his mortuary temple.

The construction of a pyramid was undertaken only by a king who had enormous power and authority. Every family in the country contributed to the project, providing either labour or food for the workers. As far as we know, they seem to have done so willingly. The king was Egypt's own god – without him the nation would not exist.

The great pyramids at Giza points towards the sky, the final resting place of their royal builders.

Pyramid city

A pyramid did not stand alone and isolated in the desert. It was at the heart of a huge complex of other buildings and facilities. Close to the main pyramid were the mortuary temple, priests' houses, storerooms and workshops. Nearby the king sometimes built smaller pyramids for his wives, mother and sisters.

While the pyramids and temple were being built, a whole 'pyramid city' of houses, bakeries, breweries and stores was needed for the thousands of workers. To keep an eye on things, the king had a specially-built palace on the same site.

Steps to smooth sides

King Djoser built the first pyramid around 2650 BC. Known as the Step Pyramid of Saqqara, it consisted of layers of stone blocks piled up like a huge cake. King Sneferu (about 2600 BC) built the first smooth-sided pyramid, the Red Pyramid. But before this, when his first attempt had started to collapse, its angles were changed mid-construction to form the Bent Pyramid.

The largest and most solid pyramids, like Khufu's or Khafre's at Giza, were constructed of solid stone blocks. To save cost, later pyramids were rubble-filled. King Amenemhet III (1922–1878 BC) built his pyramid of mud brick cased in limestone. Later, the stone was stolen and the bricks collapsed into the shapeless heap known as the Black Pyramid.

A cross-section of the Great Pyramid at Giza.

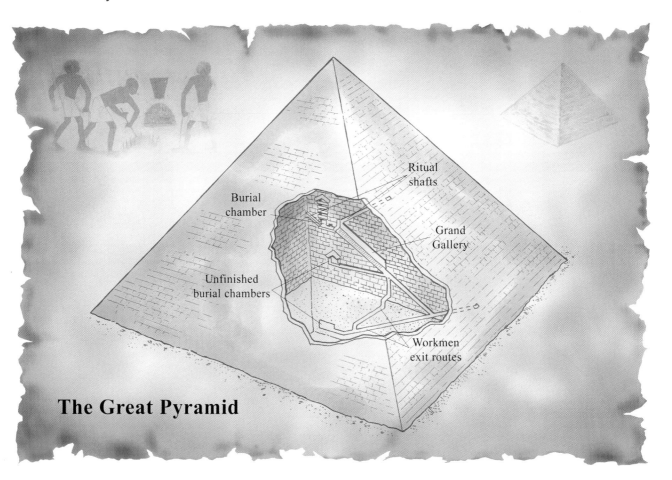

Ritual shafts

Burial chamber

Grand Gallery

Unfinished burial chambers

Workmen exit routes

The Great Pyramid

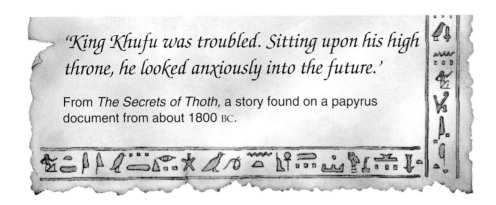

'*King Khufu was troubled. Sitting upon his high throne, he looked anxiously into the future.*'

From *The Secrets of Thoth*, a story found on a papyrus document from about 1800 BC.

When the power of the king and the wealth of his kingdom declined, as happened at the end of the Old Kingdom, fewer and smaller pyramids were built. Middle Kingdom pyramids were less solidly built, and by about 1630 BC the age of pyramid building was over.

Sleds and sweat

About 18,000 workers were employed on one of the large Giza pyramids. Most, including skilled masons and quarry men, worked all the year round. During the Nile flood season, when the fields were under water, farmers came to help at the pyramid site. The 'Overseer of All the King's Works' masterminded the whole operation.

Local limestone was used for most of the building. It was quarried by hammering wooden wedges into the stone. When water was poured onto the wedges, the wood expanded and cracked the rock. Huge blocks were cut out with wooden mallets and copper chisels, and dragged into position on sleds. Wood and other types of stone (granite) came by boat down the Nile. They were unloaded in specially-built harbours.

How were the multi-tonne blocks of stone raised into position? We cannot be sure, but they were almost certainly hauled on sleds up long ramps of rubble or brick. The organization and effort needed to raise the upper blocks over 100 metres above the ground is almost beyond belief.

Stairway to heaven

The pyramids date from the time when the sky god Re was the most important of the Egyptian gods. Faced with gleaming white limestone that stretched towards the sky, the pyramids were clearly connected with the Re cult. However, a vertical finger of stone – an obelisk – would seem a more obvious way of indicating the sun god. So why the pyramid shape?

The answer is suggested by an ancient pyramid text. It states that Re would make his rays firm enough for a king to walk up to heaven. As the pyramids were kings' tombs, therefore, they represented the beginning of their path to heaven above.

A soaring obelisk at Karnak. Many of these inscribed needles of stone were erected during the New Kingdom.

Benu

Scholars offer another reason for the pyramid shape. According to an ancient Egyptian myth, in the beginning there were just waters. These were represented by the god Nun. From these waters the first land rose up in the shape of a mound – the 'Divine Emerging Land'. Here the rest of the gods were born. A pyramid represented this sacred place.

At Heliopolis, a centre of sun worship, stood a cone which also represented the 'Divine Emerging Land'. It was known as *Benben*. On top of *Benben* perched the sun bird known as *Benu*. *Benu*, like the sun, rose again after it had died.

The tombs

Kings and queens were initially buried either under their pyramid (as at Djoser's Step Pyramid) or inside it (as at Khufu's Great Pyramid). Khufu changed his mind about the site of his burial chamber. There is an unfinished one under the pyramid and another unfinished one above that one. The burial chamber where his mummified body was finally laid was dug out in the middle of the pyramid.

Because royal burial chambers contained so many valuable objects, they were sealed and the entrance carefully hidden. Some kings set traps for grave robbers, too. We know the traps worked because the skeletons of their victims have been found inside royal burials.

'Anyone who touches my pyramid and my mortuary temple will be an outlaw, someone who eats himself.'

From a text found carved inside an Old Kingdom pyramid.

Inside the pyramid of Unas (about 2375–2345 BC). Unas was the first king to have the inside of his tomb carved with pyramid texts, which speeded his journey through the Underworld and his change into a star.

The Sphinx

If the pyramids are the grandest of Egypt's ancient monuments, the Sphinx at Giza is the most mysterious.

When was it built? Most scholars now agree that the gigantic sculpture was created at the same time as King Khafre's pyramid, about 4,500 years ago. They say that the weathered face of the Sphinx is that of the pyramid-building king. This idea is backed up by the Greek word 'sphinx', which may come from the ancient Egyptian meaning 'living image'.

Lion king

There are sphinxes at many of Egypt's sacred sites. They seem to be standing guard. Perhaps the Giza Sphinx, the largest of all, was built to guard the plateau where the pyramids stand?

Another idea is that the statue is an image of Khafre as master and sun god. The lion was a symbol of both the king and of the sun (Re). The Sphinx wears the royal head-dress and was originally painted and adorned with a crown and royal false beard – the beard is now in the British Museum. The ruins of a temple stand before the statue. Its main hall has twenty-four pillars. Do these represent the twenty-four hours of the sun god's life?

The Sphinx at Giza, with the pyramid of King Khafre behind it. Some people believed it was the image of Khafre but later it was regarded as the figure of Re the sun god.

Mysterious Glory

Another strange feature of the Sphinx is three small tunnels dug into it. One is behind the head, one at the side and one in the tail. No one knows what their purpose was or exactly when they were dug.

The Sphinx was always believed to possess magical powers. Prince Thutmose was said to have spoken to it in a dream. The creature promised he would become king if he repaired it and cleared the sand from its body. The prince did as he was asked and was crowned Thutmose IV. Since then countless others have wondered at the massive lion-man of the desert, the living symbol of ancient Egypt's mysterious glory.

A small sphinx at Memphis, built in the New Kingdom.

"*What animal walks on four legs in the morning, two in the afternoon and three in the evening?*"

[Answer: a human, crawling as a child, walking upright as an adult and with a stick in old age.]

The Riddle of the Sphinx, found in ancient Greek literature.

7 Uncovering Ancient Egypt

The ancient Greeks and Romans greatly respected Egyptian civilization. A visit to Egypt was an important part of a Greek's education, and Egyptian designs were all the rage in the early Roman Empire. The phrase 'the wisdom of Egypt' was widely used throughout the Classical world.

However, for centuries after the collapse of the Roman Empire in the fifth century AD, ancient Egypt was largely ignored. Passers by gawped at the pyramids and robbers smashed their way into tombs, but it was not until the late eighteenth century that Egyptian civilization began to be studied seriously. Since then Egyptologists from many countries have examined and preserved the monuments and other remains.

The Rosetta Stone

A key breakthrough in Egyptology was learning to read hieroglyphics. It began in 1799, when a French soldier came across an ancient stone used as part of a wall in Rosetta (Rashid), near Alexandria. The stone was carved

Now that Egypt is one of the world's most popular tourist destinations, its monuments are continually being repaired and restored. These women work on the ancient walls at Karnak.

with writing in Greek, hieroglyphs and demotic (a later development of hieroglyphics).

Led by pioneer Jean-François Champollion, scholars worked out that the three pieces of writing were different versions of the same thing – instructions for honouring King Ptolemy V. As they knew Greek, they were finally able to begin the slow process of mastering the complicated system of hieroglyphs. Once this was done, they could read other hieroglyphic texts and so unravel many more secrets of ancient Egypt's fascinating civilization.

Archaeology

Much of our information about ancient Egypt comes from archaeology. In Egypt's hot, dry climate materials like cloth and bone are excellently preserved. Moreover, most buildings were constructed from long-lasting mud brick and stone. Tombs – made as secure as possible, carved with valuable inscriptions and filled with household objects for the next life – are perhaps archaeologists' most valuable source of information.

The most famous tomb discovery was made on 4 November 1922. While exploring the Valley of the Kings, Howard Carter uncovered the sealed door to the tomb of King Tutankhamun. It contained not only the mummy of the king in a golden sarcophagus, but a priceless array of jewellery, furniture, boxes, statues and even chariots.

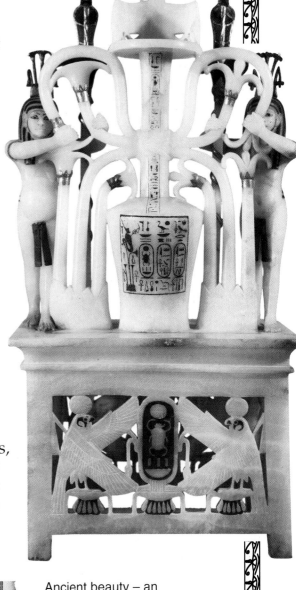

Ancient beauty – an alabaster and ivory perfume vessel from the Eighteenth Dynasty.

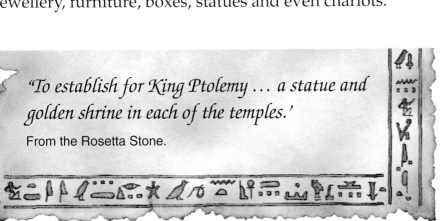

'To establish for King Ptolemy … a statue and golden shrine in each of the temples.'
From the Rosetta Stone.

The legacy

Egyptian civilization did not have a great impact on other ancient cultures. Until modern times, for example, pyramid buildings were rarely seen outside Egypt and no one else adopted hieroglyphic writing. Nevertheless, the design of the earliest Greek columns (known as Doric columns) shows Egyptian influence. Since the Renaissance, this style of architecture has spread world-wide.

Medicine is the one field of knowledge in which the Egyptians excelled. Indeed, some suggest that modern scientific medicine has its roots in ancient Egypt. Although magic played an important part in diagnosis and cure, some documents show a more practical approach. The Edwin Smith Surgical Papyrus, for example, discusses treatment of forty-eight listed injuries.

Religion

Aspects of Egyptian religion seem to have passed into Judaism, Christianity and, to a lesser extent, Islam. Parts of the Book of Proverbs and Psalm One in the Jewish Old

Homage from a Roman emperor: a kiosk (pavilion) built by the Roman emperor Trajan at the temple of Isis at Philae, near Aswan, in the first century AD. It was moved to higher ground when the Aswan dam was built in the late 1960s.

'It is bad luck to dream of being bitten by a dog: it means a spell will be cast on you.'

From the *Chester Beatty III* Papyrus.

The inside of an Egyptian coffin lid painted in the second century BC with the signs of the zodiac. The signs are still familiar in today's world.

Testament appear to be based on the Egyptian text, *The Instruction of Amenemope*. Some Hebrew words, such as those for 'reeds' and 'linen', come from ancient Egyptian words.

The mysterious cult of Isis became very popular in the Roman Empire. Aspects of Egyptian religion – for example, the idea of souls being judged after death – influenced the early Christians. It is surely no coincidence that images of Isis and the child Horus look very like those of the Virgin Mary and the infant Jesus.

Stars and signs

The division of time into hours, days and months comes from the ancient Egyptians. Their annual calendar had 365 days. Each year actually has 365 days, so their calendar coincides with ours only once every 1,460 years! This makes it very difficult to work out Egyptian dates.

The Egyptian year had twelve equal months of 30 days each. The five spare days each year, considered unlucky, were gods' birthdays. Each month was divided into three ten-day weeks.

The Egyptians realized the world was round. They also believed in the signs of the zodiac. Many of us still read our stars, just as the ancient Egyptians did: perhaps we are not so different from them after all.

Glossary

Amulet
Magic charm worn by the living and the dead.

Archaeologist
Someone who studies the past by examining physical remains.

Chant
Form of religious singing.

Complex
Group of buildings.

Cult
System of worship or belief attached to a god or goddess.

Deity
God or goddess.

Delta
Where a river spreads into several channels as it nears the sea.

Divine
Of a god or goddess.

Drought
Time of no rainfall and severe water shortage.

Dynasty
Ruling family.

Eternity
For ever and ever.

Empire
Several lands under the rule of an emperor or empress.

Granite
Very hard stone.

Hereditary
Passing on from one generation to the next.

Heresy
Belief that is against the normal religion.

Hieroglyph
Ancient Egyptian form of writing that used symbols rather than an alphabet.

Incense
Mixture that gives off a pleasant smell when burned.

Inscription
Piece of writing, carved in wood or stone.

Lower Egypt
Northern Egypt.

Mummy
Preserved corpse.

Natron
Mixture of sodium carbonate and sodium bicarbonate.

Obelisk
Tall, narrow monument of stone.

Papyrus
Tough river reed. The stems were made into a type of paper, also called papyrus.

Pharaoh
Originally the king's 'great house'. Later, it was used to mean the person from the great house – the king himself.

Phoenix
Mythical bird that arose from its own ashes.

Plateau
Level land on the top of hills or mountains.

Pylon
Large temple gateway.

Quarry
Place where building stone is dug from the earth.

Renaissance
Development of arts in Western Europe, from the late fourteenth century onwards, associated with renewed interest in ancient Greece, Egypt and Rome.

Resin
Sap of a tree.

Ritual
Important or significant action done regularly over and over again.

Sanctuary
Place where a holy image is kept.

Sarcophagus
Stone coffin.

Scribe
Someone skilled at writing.

Shrine
Place of worship of a god or goddess.

Stonemason
Someone who cuts and carves stone.

Upper Egypt
Southern Egypt.

Time Line

All dates are BC and approximate only.

7000–5500	Neolithic Age.
5500–3150	Predynastic Period. Badarians settle in Upper Egypt. Hieroglyphic writing begins.
3150–2690	Archaic Period (Dynasties 1 & 2). King Namer unites Upper and Lower Egypt.
2690–2180	Old Kingdom (Dynasties 3–6).
2650	King Djoser builds Step Pyramid.
2600	King Sneferu builds smooth-sided Red Pyramid.
2570	Khufu builds Great Pyramid at Giza.
2540	Khafre builds the Sphinx. Wars against Nubians and Libyans.
2180–2055	First Intermediate Period (Dynasties 7–10).
2055–1650	Middle Kingdom (Dynasties 11–14).
1880	King Amenemhet II builds Black Pyramid.
1650–1550	Second Intermediate Period (Dynasties 15–17).
1630	Pyramid building ends. Bronze introduced.
1550–1070	New Kingdom (Dynasties 18–20). Reigns of Hatshepsut, Thutmose III and Tutankhamun.
1464	Hatshepsut's mortuary temple built. Tombs built in the Valley of the Kings. Temple of Amenhotep III built at Luxor.
1220	Rameses II builds his Ramesseum mortuary temple.
1070–747	Third Intermediate Period (Dynasties 21–24). Conquest by Nubians.
747–332	Late Period (Dynasties 25–30). Conquest by Assyrians and Persians.
332–305	Conquest by Alexander the Great. Macedonian Dynasty.

Further Information

Books for children:
An Ancient Egyptian Child by J. Fletcher (Working White, 1999)
Daily Life of Ancient Egyptians by B. Brier (Greenwood, 1999)
People Who Made History in Ancient Egypt by J. Shuter (Hodder Wayland, 2000)
The Ancient Egyptians by J. Shuter (Hodder Wayland, 1998)
The Awesome Egyptians by T. Deary (Scholastic, 1997)
A Visitor's Guide to Ancient Egypt by L. Sims (Usborne, 2000)
Exploring Ancient Egypt by John Malam (Evans, 1999)

Books for older readers:
Ancient Egypt edited by D. Silverman (Duncan Baird, 1997)
Atlas of Ancient Egypt by J. Baines and J. Malek (Facts on File, 1983)
The British Museum of Ancient Egypt by S. Quirke and J. Spencer (Thames and Hudson, 1996)
The Egyptians by C. Aldred (Thames and Hudson, 1998)

Internet sites:
Browse with care! While there are some excellent sites on ancient Egypt, there are also some inaccurate ones. You may like to start with these.
http://www.guardians.net/egypt
http://www.clpgh.org/cmnh/exhibits/egypt
http://www.ancientegypt.co.uk/menu.html
http://www.nemes.co.uk

Places to visit:
The British Museum, London, UK, the Metropolitan Museum, New York, USA and the Cairo Museum in Egypt, have excellent exhibits on ancient Egypt. Of course, a visit to the many sites in Egypt itself will give you a wonderful insight into that country's spectacular past.

Index